Murmurs in Rhymes

Priyadarshika Ingle

BookLeaf Publishing

India | USA | UK

Presentation by *BookLeaf Publishing*

Web: www.bookleafpub.com

E-mail: info@bookleafpub.com

ISBN: 9789360948818

First edition 2025

DEDICATION

To my mother and sister, whose quirks, criticism, and love lay the foundation for my creativity.

To my friends and mentors, whose encouragement gave me the strength to carry on.

To the muses and moments that invoked delicate verses like the soft murmur of the ocean and brought me closer to feeling eternal, unconditional, and deep love.

And to you, dear reader...

These poems are now yours to read and cherish.

I place them gently before you, hoping every stanza echoes the whispers of your soul.

ACKNOWLEDGEMENT

To the wonderful team at Bookleaf—you've taken glimpses from my imagination and carefully molded them into something beautiful and tangible. I can't thank you enough for your endless patience through a series of edits. I will forever cherish your role in bringing this book into the world.

PREFACE

Everything begins with an idea. Those who hold on to that figment of their imagination and mull over it, find a way to make it real.

This book is a collection of the poems that I have clung to for the longest time. They took me on surreal journeys as I wrote and rewrote them and murmured on repeat. Thus the name.

I hope that these pages will speak to you in ways that are deeply felt.

1

Another Night

And another night holds
Only your thoughts
In its massive palms
Till the crack of dawn

It will then hand them over
Ever so gently to daytime
To oscillate
Match their fate

With the rhythm of my heart engulfed by a
million delicate butterflies fluttering in my
ribcage

As if they belong there...
As if they are home...

I might
If I'm lucky
Catch a wink during the transition

Right now
Your thoughts are too heavy to resist
Right now
I surrender once more

2

Let It Fall

Let it fall
The armor
It's OK to drop the shield
Let it out
The cry
That will make space for peace
Let your innermost thoughts drizzle sometimes
Sometimes rage like thunderous storm
Breathe
Let it flow
Believe
The journey will set you free

3

Loneliness

An emotion that salivates on your emptiness
Nibbles on your thoughts
Chomps through your brain
Chews on your heart
And starts devouring you slowly
Till you do something about it

Dear Luna

Dear Luna,

I trust your craters still hold the messages I left
The cumulonimbuses will pick them up at their
convenience
Keep them away from the orbiters and rovers for
me, will you?
And I hope they don't bother Mr. Shoemaker
either
When they arrive and mask you for a while
Please hand them all
And Mr. Sun will do his thing on the side
We've an agreement, them and I
Who else will carry and drizzle them
Where he resides?

Yours sincerely
Luminara Miles

5

My Sun

Night falls and my sun bids adieu
Leaving a muted moon staring at me
My friends... he took them too
Butterflies, birds, and bees
My world... it stopped too
Breathing for a while
Before it let out a long sigh
Aye... teasing the night
Before filling another day
With its irresistible shine

6

Recurring Glint

In the quietude of the night
I couldn't help but let my emotions pour into
this letter
I hope it will make way to you one day
My heart echoes the whispers of ageless
affection with every breath I take

We are separated by the embrace of the cosmic
canopy
Dark and velvety
But if you happen to navigate through the misty
ordeals of life all alone and need a companion
Recall our soul tie
Pull over and look at the sky

Somewhere behind the cherished ones
Will I be present
I may not be visible immediately
Because I am distant
But if you look a little carefully
And I pray that you do
You will see a recurring glint ever so gentle

That will be me...
Dimming my longing but wishing you well
Hoping you will shine a light
Leave a cue
That you're thinking about me too

7

Fireball

It is enough
The crack you left for me
My love radiates better through small spaces you
see
Now make room beyond the wall you built
Be ready for the spark, the flint
Followed by magnificence
I'm flaunting my flamboyance
No secrets, no regrets
It is not for the timid after all
To be with a fireball

Pieces

She gathered pieces of him whenever they met
As memories to treasure in her books and never
forget
She placed them carefully between the most
important pages of her life
And saw him return her love in unusual ways to
her surprise
One that rose from a genuine place deep inside
his heart
That felt her pain their distance impart

Occasionally
She visited those pages and scribbled on them
Unaware
She turned those scribbles into verses for him
Unconsciously
She choked on some delicate lines
That made her heart plead for signs
And in the muffled sobs, she quietly sighed,
"Will you not affirm that everything is alright?"

9

Miserable Heart

Must she dwell in a broken heart
After giving it away?

I know
She did mend it
Resuscitated it multiple times
Without aid

When she offered it
It was healed and whole
Wholesome, I'd say
Isn't it enough that it's gone?
Taken
And in her, it no longer stays

So there's no question about it turning cold
She is heartless, she's often told

Yes
She is, my friend
They smashed and broke it
When to the world she gladly lent it
And now she walks the planet without one
The miserable mass she has finally shunned

10

Her Poems

He forgot to take them when he robbed her of
herself
They are now lying lifeless in her diary
Like she is in limbo
Fazed with what has fizzled out
Closer to the ground
Because getting up might mean another fall
She recalls
How painful it was the last time
So she'll lie there just a little more
Shut her eyes just a little more
Choke on her salty Niles just a little more
Till she musters the courage
To birth new rhymes

11

Turbulence

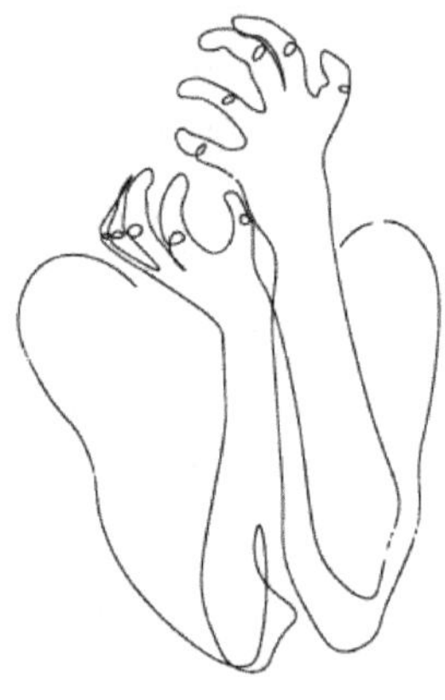

I want this turbulence to end
Because it does not make sense
That my heart is full every time I see you
And I have no place to pour those feelings out
and start anew

Sometimes I do get pockets of peace
Zen... calm
And swiftly realize
That I've entered the eye of the storm

The swirling wind ensures its brevity
With arms wide open it comes in strong
Making haste to pull me back in
Entirely... uniformed

Love might persuade me to stay
But not my pride
I can't stash my hurt away
And by your heartlessness I cannot abide

Yes
I want this turbulence to end
So some things transcend

12

A Drop I Treasured

Your eyes moistened
But you tried to beam donning rosé
Something tore at your heartstrings
I caught a drop and treasured it that day
It's the most mesmerizing thing in the world
That smile on your face
Your deep eyes soften
When a gentle curve it makes

13

True Colors

Shhhh
Listen...
The breeze whispers the secrets of the forest
The bear cared the least that the cunning fox
went for it
He devoured the honey before the bees buzzed
and stung to chase him away
They followed him across the river and past the
lion's cave
No Mowgli here to enter a barter trade
Bagheera is a stranger
Far from being a friend

This jungle displays
The true colors of the modern day
Where people amidst people
Live as they're cast away

14

The Greater Enchantment

Their thoughts all day
Keep your mind consumed
Curious feelings at play
Are they at their end too?

You hit the sack
Overwhelmed furthermore
But to the dreamworld and back
Recall fuzzy kittens, books galore

Dawning upon you thus
That the adoration is an entrapment
And the dream you dreamed
Is the greater enchantment

15

Luna

She rides the crescent
Shooting arrows of stars
She ties the present
With stories from afar
Goddess, Chandra, Iah, Selene
Several names for one celestial being
Being. Yes, being...
'cos she breathes
She shines her light sometimes only for me
To chase away my gloomy dreams
In alternate realities
Stealing my anxiety
When I move between the worlds
Promising me she'll be there
For better or for worse

16

Breaking My Fast

Breaking my fast
To replenish my endlessly
Starving body by
Relishing a slice of my
Aching heart stabbed cruelly

17

Drifting Away

If it's time for me to drift away
Please expect no lines from me
Days will pass and so will weeks
With no words in this wicked reality

But I can't be sure
Of what the seasons would transform
It sure does seem
Like they will stir up a storm

So pardon me
If I get wistful when it rains
Or I yearn for your warmth
In the soulless chill

Forgive me
If I never return
To revive the decaying dreams
That you once killed

18

Relentless Pursuit

She's had the desire to traverse the planet
Holding her journals close to her bosom she
plans it
Some cash stuffed in her potli
Tucked in properly
Next to a silver chhallah on her waist
Hidden under her khadi palla and away
She goes
Relentless
Egos
Pointless
Treads
With purpose
Despite being guided
By a broken compass

19

The Sky Last Night

The sky last night
Tempted me to capture its brilliance
Did you see it too?

I tucked sweet messages
In the silken swaying clouds
And the craters of the moon

Its moonshine
Shimmered
Shimmered coming through

The stars
Witnessed a miracle
When it embraced me in its divine hue

20

27

Festivities and Feasts

It's the calm before the festivities
And the fasts before the feasts

21

Loving Grief

She deciphered his silence
And agreed to part ways
Not escape
Her love for him was true always
Distance maybe to start anew
He did too
Very ungracefully I must say

He painted a lasting masterpiece for a moment
Of warm desires as she had of him
But they were destined to follow their precious
dreams

Carrying ribs with half-filled hollows and
muffled screams

So together they hiked their last mile
To soak in the serenity of their silence for the
last time
Lose themselves in their soulful eyes
Melt in their warm embrace while
Destiny conspired to add a touch of whimsy to
their lives
It put him in front of her again
In a silent cave
Unexplained
Turned a pleasant surprise into
An emotional hurricane
And this time...

They smiled as though whispering sweet lies
Gasped for another breath drowning in the
deepest depths of their eyes
Allowed their brimming ache to flow
Before reaching out and holding hands under
quiet sighs
Till it was time for them to leave
With hearts full of loving, loving grief

22

Divinity

The distant
Echoes of muffled
Mrudang taal
Songs and hymns
Carried by the south-west winds
Under wispy skies

Not Enough

A dreamy poem
Lived only from dawn to dusk
Is just not enough

24

Peaks and Shores

You cannot
Not admire the mountains
From the sunken realms

You cannot
Not allow the murmurs fill your ears
Where the sea meets the shore overwhelmed

25

Off Late

Your energy I emulate
Exceeding my state
But don't worry, my love
We will be even someday
It takes time to give my worst off late

26

His Eyes

She could drown in them
His eyes
Deep
Brown
Beautiful
Hypnotic eyes
That sparkle only for her
When he smiles

27

Pine Tops

Tapering pine tops
Prodding the misty skyline
Fading with distance
Till only fogginess lasts
Over its fine existence

28

The Celestial Ride

The celestial chariot lingered
While the moon poured its aching desire and
triggered
Dazzling cascades
Beneath the veil of unseen gaze
Till it graced the endless sands
And caressed the silver waves

29

Elegant Need

I wait...
As time stands still
In silence...
It may seem
For I gulp down any word
That wants to escape me
My love may never speak
Even though it has a million ways
To express its elegant need

30

Be All Smiles

Be all smiles, my love
Be all smiles
And you'll turn any passage
Into golden miles

31

For the Nth Time

For the nth time
Love swells the heart of my heart
Bursting
Radiating light
Pure
White
But with a slight
Ache

For the nth time
It's floating in the ether
And I wonder if you'd ever
Feel the pulse
And describe
My pain

32

Silent a Lifetime

Her cry pierces through
The unstirred air that had been
Silent a lifetime

33

Between Words & Worlds

Between words
He's free to teleport
To a different world
Where he's writing his own story
The way it hasn't been written here
Holding something close
Letting something go
But beyond it all
Just being the gentlest of souls

34

Like Mist

It's that time, my love
When it feels like
The clouds and the drizzles
The sneaky sunshine over our castles
Seek and hide till
Miss Selene emanates her beams
That kind of struggle passing through the dense
Sama trees
At a distance that almost feels
Reachable like
The glinting stars
Strewn everywhere I glance
Mischievously winking
Leaving not a single chance
To tease me

They come along and of you
They remind me
Before disappearing for hours
Leaving a pining heart
And the stifled verses my lips once kissed
Of your thoughts floating in it like mist

35

Oh, Universe!

Oh, Universe!
I declare to thee
Break these shackles
And forever set me free
Bring me face-to-face
With my purpose finally
One that seeks and desires me
In my entirety
I declare to thee
That at the count of three
Make this wish for once
My reality
One, two, THREE!

36

Aflame Hearts

Do you have the courage to enter the dragon's
lair
Embrace the burning desires I dare
Let 'em burst into flames—your bodies and
brains
That you tamed and trained
To canoodle the mundane
Till only aflame hearts remain
And you're no longer loving in vain

37

Before Spring Bloom

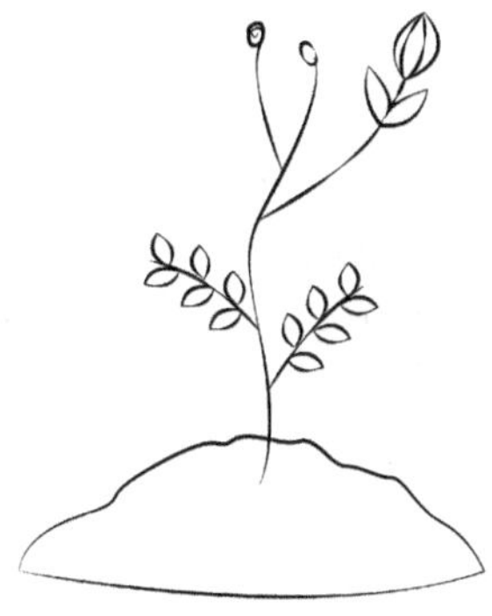

Life goes on or so it seems
While her mind is full of him and his memories
Who knows
If it's she who is caught in their cage or them in
her's
Her eyes may never give away what she truly
feels

But sometimes in the cold hours of quietude
She lets it trickle—the old distress
Her soul whispers a silent prayer
That he'd remember her in the littlest of things
he encounters every day

The droplets of her bleeding heart may be wiped
away
The wound may slowly heal
His face in her mind—sketched and erased
Since time immemorial

What will never cease to exist through this
ordeal
Is the little voice inside her appeal
"I wish you'd come back soon
At least before spring bloom"

38

Tropical Monsoon

A serene sun
A blazing moon
The clouds ashen
In eternal June

Light dissolves
As darkness falls
The heart sings
A melancholic tune

"Cross over. Come hither"
The voices urge in unison
But I remain dampened in time
Still... drunk on the tropical monsoon

39

Wildflower

Be the wildflower you're meant to be
You don't need permission to bloom
You do you at your own pace
When it's right for you
Not when there's room

You're colorful
Fragrant
Incessantly beautiful
Untamed

Let them look at you and wonder
How you filled the earthy hive
What's upon you
That in the darkness you survived

You were manifested
Your seed the earth embraced
The wilderness
Invested

You're one with them now coz you trusted their
instincts
You trust the wild shrubs you blossom in
You count on the bees and birds that drink your
nectar sweet still
You bank on the thorns who protect you and die
a little when you wilt...

Wilt... gracefully...
Effusing your delightful fragrance...
Wildflower

40

Every Evening

"Give them back to me!"
Demands the ocean as the sun rises every
morning
"I will," the sun says
"As soon as I kiss you goodnight, my darling"
And every evening he moves closer
And every evening she blushes pink
And every evening the sun dies
To return her velvety starlit skies

41

Whispers of Devotion

The moon shone his brilliance
Swelling the ocean
Who birthed waves in whispers
Confessing her devotion

42

The Queen of Shadows

The Queen's silhouette levitates midair
Leading her ton of shadows
Her entourage of victorious wolves
Departing crimson meadows
She'll be gone sooner than you know
Abandoning those who are callow
It's your last chance to bear
Your unseen scars from the darkest hollows

43

Him Vs Her

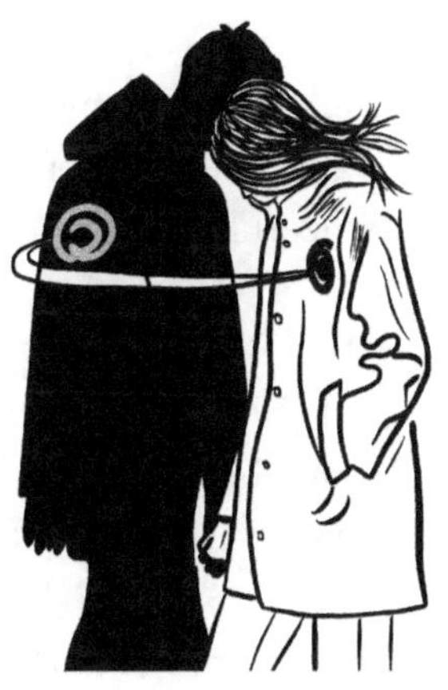

When his curiosity wounded her pride
Her temper hurt his bashfulness
Now uneasiness visits
When fate brings them together
He hesitates
She looks away
"I know your game," she thinks
"So it is…" he concludes, it seems

It's best to shun the other
Both presume
Maybe it's unrequited

Both assume
And neither look nor smile
Is what they did for a while
Till indifference dissolved into the ether
Her heart then ached, tethered
To the memories, the desires

And again, she's engulfed by a slurry of
thoughts and emotions
Her mind and her heart have set things in motion
He…
Bears nothing
He probably isn't in pain
Or maybe he is too
And pretends to be sane

And while this goes on, she almost screams
"I detest it! I detest this pulsing unease
Murmurs stirred about our spirits
They were destined to meet
Curiosity piqued when your eyes, unwavering,
sought mine
And when you broke your gaze in a fleeting
breath… why?
Why did you do that?
What made you act so
Without a word to spare?
What whispered in your heart
That you left me in despair?"

44

55

A Gentle Word

A gentle word
Can birth
A village of hearts
Willing
To surrender to your purpose
Willing
To echo your strength

45

Hydrangeas and Dahlias

Beautiful hydrangeas
Fuchsia and dahlias
Hummingbirds and butterflies
Drinking sweet nectar and I
Feel like they should always be
Around the flowers and also me

46

The Crack Willow

Mountain ranges rising
In the lake's western shore
Snowy peaks reaching
Six thousand feet and more
Amid serene waters
Is a delicate Wanaka tree
Not the sole attraction
But admirers come to see
How she stands
While she can
Like it's a splendid wonder
Old and fragile
The crack willow can't blunder
Broken and battered
Can you hear her creak?
Yet tirelessly
She carries on you see
It seems her friends have sworn
To assist till it's time
The muddy floor holds her bough
When the waters rise fine
And "Leave her be. Leave her be."

I hear the breeze whisper
When the pirates ascend in the darkest trend
And she lets out a soft whimper

47

They

They come around
Every once in a while
Blurting words that prick and pierce
For they cannot see you living with pride
Being what they never thought you'd
be—FIERCE!

Do you want to be blind
Despite witnessing the truth?
Do you want to be deaf
When the answers come through?
Do you want to bend
And let them walk all over you?

They are dull
Dull and weak
Blaming the dead
Who cannot speak
Defaming your own

Can't you see?

Their pale bulging eyes and smirks
Their narrow minds choked with dirt
Their hearts—stone cold, filled with greed
Sowing the seed
Of doubt that might sprout
But it's on you
To not let it grow into a tree

48

Jolly Grant

It was the 24th of a scorching summer month
Jolly Grant abuzz with whines and grunts
Leisure, adventure, business, spiritual break
Every nomad had a plan till the flights were
delayed

With no seats, I caught a corner on the floor
Beside a 20-something wandering spirit,
handsome and sure
Kindle out; batteries checked
Eyes darting at the boarding gate

The glass wall gave a hopeful view
But the crowd panicked soon
And how to cut those hours
I had no clue

The lad started a conversation out of the blue
And for hours we spoke and shared our food
Till shifting plans became crucial
With separate paths to pursue, we bid each other
adieu

I guess this is one of the perks of travelling
alone
We're a little with everyone even though we're
on our own

49

A Joyous Melody

The ceoltóir played a joyous melody
And every single passerby
Carried a piece of it along
Some in hums
Some in the spring in their step
Skipping
Holding hands
Twirling
Smiles abound
Sparkling eyes
I can see it
Can you, too?

50

Much Like Gold

Fed by a gushing river
Lined by a forest
A long way up where it's cold
A lake sparkles with glassy whispers
Amid yellow flowers I'm told

A soothing breeze softly whistles
The sun gleams through the pines
Scattering its light manifold
Glistening, shimmering
Much like gold

51

I Am the Light

So they say that time heals
Blurs certain images etched in memories
Therefore I walk the path with all my heart
Somedays needing to muster the courage to dart
Through extreme feelings of joy brimming
Choking gloom
Withdrawal that left mountains of ache
Fiery rage

Several nudges it takes
To refrain from letting randos waltz in and steal
my light
Several notes I make
To remind me that I am made unusual
Of dreams they will seldom see
Precious; valuable
Of dust from the stars and pixies
Glowing; ethereal

I am the light they were gripped by
They falsified brutally
And slipped by
I am the piece of heaven their hungry souls bit
into
Gnawed and chewed but mind you
Their encased hearts thick with grime
May relish the flavor
But cannot assimilate the divine

52

A Moment in Their Skin

No matter what the state of your soul is
Carve out time to wander through poems
Sulk through the stanzas
Rage through the verses
Love through every word passionately inscribed
Allow the poet's thoughts to weave into yours
You are meant to be them, if just for a heartbeat